Also by Jill Krementz

*The Face of South Vietnam*
(WITH TEXT BY DEAN BRELIS)

*Sweet Pea—A Black Girl*
*Growing Up in the Rural South*

*Words and Their Masters*
(WITH TEXT BY ISRAEL SHENKER)

*A Very Young Dancer*

*A Very Young Rider*

*A Very Young Gymnast*

*A Very Young Circus Flyer*

*A Very Young Skater*

*The Writer's Image*

*How It Feels When a Parent Dies*

*How It Feels to be Adopted*

*How It Feels*
*When Parents Divorce*

*Jill Krementz*

# *How It Feels*
# *When Parents Divorce*

*Alfred A. Knopf  New York*

*19*  *84*

THIS IS A BORZOI BOOK
PUBLISHED BY ALFRED A. KNOPF, INC.

Library of Congress Cataloging in Publication Data
Krementz, Jill.
How it feels when parents divorce.
Summary: Boys and girls, ages seven to sixteen,
share their feelings about their parents' divorce.
1. Children of divorced parents—Interviews—
Juvenile literature.
2. Divorced parents—Juvenile literature.
3. Parents and child—Juvenile literature.
[1. Divorce]   I. Title.
HQ777.5.K73   1984      306.8'9      83-48856
ISBN 0-394-54079-4

Manufactured in the United States of America
First Edition

*This book is dedicated*
*to*
*John Woodside*
*with my thanks*

# Introduction

First, I want to say how much I like and admire the families you are about to meet. Even though they have all experienced the shattering displacement of divorce, they have survived as parents —and as children. They may not live together any longer, but they can still talk to one another—and allow one another to be heard. The voices in this book belong to the children, but behind each of the nineteen stories there are mothers and fathers and step-parents who have not only permitted but, more importantly, have encouraged each child to speak honestly and from the heart. These are not anonymous stories; these children's real names have been used and they have allowed themselves to be photographed. It took courage for them to talk openly about their fears, their sorrows, their confusions, knowing full well that what they were revealing about themselves would not only be read by strangers but by the very people whose actions had caused much of their pain.

But I think they all believed—as I do—that sharing their own histories and feelings would be of real use to other children and other parents in the midst of a similar crisis in their lives. I know I myself would have been strengthened and comforted, after my own parents were divorced, by knowing that other children had experienced many of the same problems and emotions I was experiencing, and I believe that my parents would have benefited too. Though divorce must always be painful for everyone involved, there are ways that parents can alleviate that pain—and it is often the children who can best tell us what those ways are.

Jill Krementz

# Contents

# *Zach, age thirteen*

Even though I live with my Dad and my sister lives with my Mom, my parents have joint custody, which means we can switch around if we feel like it. I think that's the best possible arrangement because if they had fought over us, I know I would have felt I was like a check in a restaurant—you know, the way it is at the end of a meal when two people are finished eating and they both grab for the check and one says, "I'll pay it," and the other one says, "No, this one is mine," and they go back and forth, but secretly neither one really wants it, they just go on pretending until someone finally grabs it, and then that one's stuck.

It's kind of nice the way it is because whenever I want to see my other parent I can, and if I have a fight with one of them, instead of having to take off and stay with friends or hang out on the street, I can just go eat at my Mom's house or my Dad's, whatever the case may be, and I think that's good. But it has its drawbacks, too. The other kids all seem to have their opinions about joint custody, and they always feel free to give me their opinions, which maybe I don't want to hear. For example, it does raise eyebrows whenever I tell people that I'm living with my Dad, because traditionally the mother gets the kids and the father gets to pay alimony and stuff, which my parents don't do. My Mom said she had too much pride to take alimony and she wanted to make it on her own, so that's our way and I admire her for it. My friends will say dumb things like "What's wrong with your Mom that you don't live with her?" Things like that. It gets me very upset.

I hate it when I see movies or hear stories about how bad divorce is and how the dad is always getting the bum deal, because kids belong to fathers as much as mothers and it isn't always the man's fault. It seems that men always have to be penalized by having to pay alimony or having the kids taken away from them. It's not fair for one person to stomp out, complaining about all the things that were wrong. I went to a camp once and the most important thing I learned was that if you consistently find yourself having problems with other people, you ought to take a close look at yourself to see what you might be doing wrong. Even if you do think the other person is being selfish, self-centered, opinionated, and unloving, you still have to see which of the problems you yourself are causing. You also have to consider the possibility that some of the problems are being caused by outside things—say, by pressures. It also helps to remind yourself that you're probably complaining about relatively small problems compared to important things like the situation in Cambodia—like maybe the wife is complaining that her husband doesn't kiss her goodnight, when that same evening in Cambodia people are going to bed without any food to eat.

My parents knew they couldn't live together, but they also knew it was nobody's fault. It was as if they were magnets—as if when you turn them the opposite way they can't touch. They themselves said that they got married for all the wrong reasons and weren't really thinking what it was going to be like ten years from then. They're just two totally different people with very different temperaments. Neither of them ever blamed the other person, so they worked it out the best they could—for their sakes and ours, too.

Nevertheless, it's very sad and confusing when your parents are divorced. I think I was five when they separated and that it was another two or three years before they made it official, but I'm not really sure. All I know for certain is that it was a long time ago and since then my sister and I have lived in a *lot* of places. First we lived with our Mom, and then when I was in second grade she moved away to live with a boyfriend, so we lived with our Dad for a year. Then Mom and her boyfriend broke up, so she got her own apartment and we were with her sort of part-time but we lived more with our Dad. The year after that, my Mom came back to where my Dad was living, and my Dad moved to another apartment and we lived with my Mom. Then my Mom moved to the country for a year because she wanted to write a book, and I went with her to the country. But my sister stayed with my Dad. After that, my parents started living together again, even though they were divorced—they did it mostly for my sister's and my sake—but it didn't work, so they moved apart again and my Dad moved back into his original apartment. I moved in with him, and my sister went with my Mom, who rented an apartment only a few blocks away. For a

while it used to be a very loose arrangement—if my sister and I felt like switching, we could. But now my sister wants to stay with my Mom, and I like living with my Dad because all my stuff is there and I've sort of prettied up my room. I've got six birds, and if I moved out, I wouldn't be able to keep them because Mom's place is too small.

What's too bad is that in a way I feel sort of divorced from my sister. Of course we would probably have killed one another if we had actually lived together for the past few years, but still, now that we're older she's nice to be around and we can talk more to each other instead of fighting all the time. Even though we're neighbors, we don't get to see each other all that much because we each have so much homework and we both have sports and our parents each have jobs and we're all so busy that we're all kind of watching out for ourselves.

When my parents first split up, it affected me a lot—much more than my sister. I got real fat and my grades went way down, so I went to a psychologist. She made me do a lot of things which seemed dumb at the time—like draw pictures and answer lots of silly questions, like what kind of animal would I be if I was an animal. Well, I told her I'd be a crocodile because he could eat anything he wanted. At that time, food was security, and that's what I needed, which is why I was eating nonstop. My school work suffered because I was so distracted thinking about my situation that I couldn't listen very well, and for a long time I didn't work nearly as hard as I should have. Everyone told me I was an underachiever, and my parents tell me I still am, but I don't think so. What I do think is that I am a lot more independent—a go-out-and-do-it-yourself person.

But there are drawbacks in that. Like I've gotten so used to doing things by myself now that I can't do anything with anybody else. I'm very individualized, whatever you call it. I'll give you one situation. There's this guy who's my biggest enemy in the whole school. He's loud, he's wild, he's rough, he's huge, and he's a slob. I mean, he's anything you can think of. One time we were playing two-hand touch and he came up behind me, which is offsides and real, real illegal, and he tackled me. I just freaked out all over him. I had no self-control at all. And this past summer when I went to camp, we took a five-day canoe trip and I was bowman. Well, no matter how hard my stern man paddled, I kept yelling at him to paddle harder. I felt like my mind was on fire the whole time—I was just ready to kill the poor guy. I have a real hard time dealing with other people in team sports. I far prefer doing things alone—like playing tennis or wrestling.

The one time of year when I wish my parents weren't divorced is Christmas. That's because I have this Bing Crosby image of a "White Christmas" type of family—Mr. and Mrs. Smith and Bobby Smith and Sally Smith all sitting around a beautiful Christmas tree with nice lights and a fire going and Bing Crosby crooning in the background and Mr. Smith reciting " 'Twas the Night Before Christmas." In our family it's "Oh, what do you want for Christmas?" and we all go over to my Mom's because she's got the decorations, but I think, Wow! I never really have the family experience.

I feel the same way at some of our school events, too. We don't have a Parents Day, but we do have a lot of other stuff—like

Field Day—where all the little family comes, and I just tell my parents not to bother because I always, always feel awkward and stiff when the family is together. I prefer for just one of my parents to come—like last year, when I was in a play. My Dad came one time and my Mom came another, and it was no big deal. But when they both come, it's a bigger deal than it should be and I feel strange—especially at the end of the event, because my Mom will want to do something like kiss my Dad good-night while he's trying to walk away, and I just think it makes him feel embarrassed. You see, my Mom is always kind of happy-go-lucky—I guess you can call it charming—and my Dad's more serious and definitely more moody, so I can sense a real tenseness when we all go out and try to do things together.

My Mom says she'd never get remarried—her feeling is, why bother with the title of "married" when you can just live with somebody? For her, marriage is too confining. My Dad, on the other hand, would very much like to get remarried and have some more children, which is okay with me as long as I don't have to baby-sit too much. I hope my Dad doesn't wait too long, though, because he's almost forty, and if, say, it was ten years from now, I'd kinda feel sorry for the kid because he's got this Dad who can't go out and play ball with him. I've got some friends who've got older dads, and the kids aren't very good athletes. Maybe they should play with other kid's dads. That's what I should have done when I was in the fourth grade and living with my Mom. I used to hang around the shopping mall instead of playing sports, and I'd probably be a better athlete today if I'd been more resourceful. It was just that I was at the age when I was sort of relying on my Dad to be there.

I've heard about kids who have all these problems because their parents are getting divorced, but I can't understand what the big deal is. I mean, it's upsetting, sure, but just because your parents are separated it doesn't mean you're going to lose anybody. Your parents might not be together, but they're still going to be there when you need them. Maybe I feel that way because I was only five when mine split. Who knows, maybe if I'd been older I would have gotten all angry and screwed up like other kids I hear about. It's not something I talk about very much. Most of my friends would rather talk about MTV than talk about divorce.

In some ways it's good that divorce is getting so common, because it's getting more modernized—you know, not just the wife

always getting the kids. And it's getting to be more accepted because society is growing and changing and divorce isn't a dirty word anymore. It's still not a *clean* word, because it has a menacing sound, but it is cleared as a normal, everyday—whatever—thing that happens. Of course *marriage* is a lot happier word than *divorce*, but I do think it's understood now that marriage is more casual and less of a permanent arrangement than it used to be. Back in 1900 you got married and stuck it out, for better or worse, and that was it.

I read a book by Arthur C. Clarke called *Childhood's End*, which is about the future, and when people—they're called Overlords and they come to Earth from outer space—want to get married, they sign contracts for one year, or five, or ten, whatever length of time they want, and that's how long they're obligated to stay together. Some people might call this a science fiction concept of marriage, but if you ask me, it makes a lot of sense!

# *Lulu, age eight*

My parents got divorced when I was only a tiny baby, so I don't remember anything about what happened. I know that Mama was the one who left, and it was because they were fighting a lot and being mean to each other and that's not a nice way to live. I suppose they needed a divorce to be happy, but there are times when I think it was stupid and unfair and mean to me. But I know I can't do anything about it, and I'm happy the way my parents are living now, so I guess I don't really mind too much. It's mostly the *idea* of their being divorced that makes me unhappy. My mother lives with someone I like a lot. Of course there are times when I wish to myself they would get back together, but I know it won't happen, so I'm not really thinking about it.

I live with my mother and her boyfriend, Michael, and even though they're not married and even though they hardly ever fight, when they do I worry, "Oh dear, I hope they don't get into a serious argument because it could happen that they'll get divorced." I would hate for them to break up because I really think of Michael as my stepfather and I've grown to love him so much. Still, I hope they don't get married because I like it just the way it is and because I only want to have one father. And I also don't want my father to get married to his girlfriend, because if they had a child, then I would feel he wouldn't really be my father anymore. It sounds selfish, I know, but I just don't want to have a brother or sister. I like being the only one. I've told my mother that I don't want her to have another child either, but I've also said that if she has one I'm not going to complain or anything because it's not for me to say yes or no. She's free to do what she wants.

One of the sad parts of the divorce is that I don't get to see Papa as much as I'd like to. For quite a few years Mama and I lived in Europe and Papa lived in America. Then we came to New York, but Papa was working in California. I've seen more of him in the last year, but now that I've been with my mother all this time, I've grown very attached to her and I find I don't want to be away from her too much.

Not so long ago Mama and Papa took me out for dinner, and I kept hoping they would sit next to each other. I was very happy that I could see them, and only them, together, and I was wishing that it could be for more than one night. They still see each other often, but whenever they're together, usually Papa's with his girlfriend and Mama's with Michael. Sometimes I secretly wish it could just be Mama and Papa, but then I feel bad because I really love Michael and I'd hate to lose him or leave him out.

Mama says it's a mistake to live your life fearing loss because you lose people in all sorts of ways but you hold on to them in other

ways, too. She says that life is very surprising and you have to be brave and curious—when you're a brave and curious person you might just get married eight times. If you live your life afraid of loss, you're not living, you're just waiting for someone to disappoint you. Mama tells me I'll understand someday when I'm older and have more of a life and maybe even a marriage of my own. And she says parents shouldn't tell their children everything, that in time I'll figure things out on my own and either forgive her or not forgive her, or even decide that it's not a matter of forgiveness. I do think that Mama has always done the best she can, that she always has and she always will.

There's a book by Judy Blume called *It's Not the End of the World*, which is all about how two children felt about their

parents' divorce. The little girl could talk about it with her friend, but her brother didn't have anyone to talk to about his feelings, and so he ended up feeling angry and mean all the time. I don't have any friends I talk to, but I do talk to my mother since she's like a best friend and it does make me feel a lot better.

I think that when parents get divorced, they both have special responsibilities toward their children—like trying to make life as easy as possible. They should be especially kind and loving and give their kids a lot of attention and try to make up for what's happened. Mama's always doing little things to make me feel special—like one day when I came home from school around Eastertime, she was all dressed up as a bunny and hopping around the living room. She had on a pink jumpsuit with a powder puff on her bottom and socks on her hands and feet and funny bunny ears on top of her head. She's really a character. And for Christmas she made me a dollhouse. I loved it much more because she made it herself. Even Mama couldn't believe she had done it, because she doesn't think she's very good with her hands.

But the most important thing for parents to do is to help their children to understand why they got a divorce. They should let them think about the divorce as much as they want and let them ask as many questions as they feel like. My mother has told me a lot of things that have helped me—like divorce isn't anything to feel ashamed or embarrassed about. Our family motto is "Proud to Be Weird," and that's helped us through a lot.

# *Ari, age fourteen*

When my parents were married, I hardly ever saw my Dad because he was always busy working. Now that they're divorced, I've gotten to know him more because I'm with him every weekend. And I really look forward to the weekends because it's kind of like a break—it's like going to Disneyland because there's no set schedule, no "Be home by five-thirty" kind of stuff. It's open. It's free. And my father is always buying me presents.

My Mom got remarried and divorced again, so I've gone through two divorces so far. And my father's also gotten remarried—to someone I don't get along with all that well. It's all made me feel that people shouldn't get married—they should just live together and make their own agreement. Then, if things get bad, they don't have to get divorced and hire lawyers and sue each other. And, even more important, they don't have to end up hating each other.

I'd say that the worst part of the divorce is the money problem. It's been hard on my Mom because lots of times she can't pay her bills, and it makes her angry when I stay with my father and he buys me things. She gets mad and says things like "If he can buy you things like this, then he should be able to pay me." And I feel caught in the middle for two reasons: first, I can't really enjoy whatever my Dad does get for me, and second, I don't know who to believe. My Dad's saying, "I don't really owe her any money," and my Mom's saying he does. Sometimes I fight for my Mom and sometimes I fight for my Dad, but I wish they'd leave me out of it completely.

In a lot of ways I wish my Mom would get remarried, because then she wouldn't have to worry so much about finances. But I'm sorry that my Dad got remarried, because I feel left out a lot of times. And one thing I really worry about is that I think they want to have a baby, and I *know* that if they do, it will be just like a replacement for me. That's because I only see my Dad on weekends, and since he would see the baby more than he'd see me, he'd probably grow to like it more than he likes me. It could be a lot like what happened with my dog Spunkur. I've had him for about six years and I've always said I'll *never* love any dog as much as I love him. Well, a year ago I picked up a little black Labrador puppy from the pound, and now I find I'm not as friendly with Spunkur as I used to be. And I think Spunkur feels jealous, just like I would if my Dad and my step-mother had a baby. My Dad said it wouldn't be that way, that we'd be a whole family and I'd have a little brother or sister, which would be a lot of fun, but I told him, "Look, by the time the kid is old enough to talk, I'll be out of college. I'm not going to have anything to do with a baby. You know that it's just a replacement for me!"

If I lived full-time with my Dad, it would probably be easier for me to accept a baby because we'd be on an equal footing, but I'd rather stay with my Mom, where life is normal—where we live like most people live, with breakfast at breakfast time and dinner at dinner time. I do my homework, play with my friends— it's all the way life should be. If I lived with my Dad, it might be more fun at times, but I would go crazy. I wouldn't want to be brought up that way.

# *Meredith, age fourteen*

I was nine when my parents separated, and it was a total shock to me. In fact, when my father and older sister told me, I thought they were joking. I ran upstairs to ask my mother, and she told me it was true. The reason it was a complete surprise is because my parents never really argued, or if they did, they always tried to hide it from us. Sometimes they would go into the kitchen and close the door. Looking back, I suppose I knew there were problems, but I never wanted to admit it. If once in a while I actually heard them arguing, I'd say to myself, "Boy, I wonder what would happen if they got separated?" But I would always know that was never going to happen to *my* parents.

I don't remember when my father actually moved out, because sometimes he was there and sometimes he wasn't. It was like he was always moving his things around and I never really knew if he was in the house or not. One day he would be there and spend the night, and the next day he would be gone. It was very disruptive and I didn't realize until a few years later that he had moved back with us a few times, hoping to work things out.

They finally got divorced about a year later, when I was ten. My mother wasn't going to tell me, because she was trying to prove that life would be the same as when they were only separated, but I found out, anyway. I was home by myself one day and my mother's lawyer called to say they'd set the court date. So when Mom came home I gave her the message and asked if they were getting a divorce, and she said yes. I had been hoping they would get back together, so the news made me sad. Even now I still hope they'll get back together, but I realize it will never happen and I've learned to live with it.

My two sisters and I live with my mother and we go on seeing our father often, though not on a regular basis. Even when my parents were still married we didn't see him that much, because he's a police officer and he worked nights a lot. I would get up in the morning and kiss him good-bye while he was still asleep. Then I'd go to school. By the time I came home he'd be gone to work, and when he came home I'd be asleep. So the divorce didn't really affect my life in terms of not seeing my Dad. But it really affected me emotionally. I just felt bad all the time. I used to cry a lot, and when I wasn't crying I would feel like crying. Even some of my teachers noticed I was depressed—it was just a terrible time in my life. My older sister seemed to deal with it better than I did, and my younger sister didn't deal with it at all—until just last year, when she started getting stomach-aches all the time. Even though my sisters and I didn't talk much about our feelings, I know I would have felt more alone and lonely if I was an only child. In the beginning we all comforted each other. But the only thing that really helped me was time.

The divorce has brought me much closer to my mother because when I was going through the worst of it—all those times when I was crying—I talked to her a lot. My relationship with my parents has changed because now my mother does all the disciplining and sometimes she resents it—especially when we tell her how much fun we have with Dad. It's as if it's all fun and games with him because we're with him so little that there's not much we can do in those few hours to get ourselves in trouble.

I would like to see my father more than I do. In the beginning he saw me a lot, but now there are weeks when I don't see him at all, or even talk to him. I think that when parents do get divorced, whichever parent doesn't get custody should try to see his or her kids as much as possible. And I think that when people get divorced they shouldn't say bad things about each other to their kids. For example, my mother will say something like "Well, you'd better call your father this week and remind him to pick you up," as if he would forget if we didn't remind him. Those are the kind of remarks I resent. My father does it too, and I wish they both would stop.

I know that I'll get married someday. But I also know that I can't say for sure that I'm never going to get divorced. That's because my mother used to tell me that when she got married she thought that *she* wasn't going to get divorced. All I know for sure is that I'm going to try my best. Growing up with divorced parents might make me think twice. I mean, if somebody proposed to me, I might wait until I was older so I could feel more sure that the marriage would work. My parents were only twenty, and maybe things would have worked out better if they had waited a few more years.

# *Jimmy, age ten*

My mother divorced my father when I was two and a half. My Mom took me to live with her, but she couldn't cope, and so she was going to put me up for adoption. There was a big scene because my Dad didn't want that to happen, and so I went to live with him. Actually, I stayed at my grandmother's house for a couple of months because Daddy's a letter carrier and he had to leave the house at six in the morning. But he used to come and see me every day after work and we'd have dinner together. Then I moved in with him for the next three years—until the first "snatch."

What happened is that one evening my mother and her boy-friend, Don, came to take me for a weekend, and she told me to wait for her in the car while she went into the house to talk to my father. I didn't find out until later that she was telling him she was planning to keep me. All I knew was that when she and Don tried to leave with me, my Dad came running out of the house and held on to the car door as we were pulling away from the curb. He started yelling and screaming, and the neighbors

29

called the cops, who came and asked to see Daddy's custody papers. He couldn't find them, so they let me go with my mother and Don. Soon after that, my father went to a lawyer and they got everything straightened out so I could go back to living with him—actually, with him and his girlfriend, Kate. During this time, Kate and Dad got married and I kept on seeing my mother off and on for weekends. But every time my mother came to fetch me, she and my father would get into some terrible argument, and forget it, good-bye, everyone would just go crazy! It would have been nice if they could have been more civilized to each other.

It was during this time that my mother decided she wanted me back for good, and there was another big custody fight. I had to go to court and talk to the judge, and I told him I was happy where I was. I don't remember too much except that the judge told me that my mother had gotten married—to Don—and I was really surprised by the news. It hurt my feelings that she hadn't even bothered to say anything to me beforehand about her marriage. The judge said he had to think about what should happen but in the meantime I should stay where I was, so I left the court with my father. Two months later the court decided that I should live permanently with my Dad but keep on seeing my mother on weekends.

Well, that made my mother so mad that she decided to steal me. One weekend while I was visiting her, she and Don packed up their car with a lot of stuff and we all piled in. I kept asking her, "Where are we going?" And finally she said, "Take a wild guess." I guessed a couple of places and finally I said Florida because that was the one place she had talked about a lot—she had some relatives who lived there. I didn't have any idea how far away Florida was, so I asked her how long it would take us to get there, and she said about two days. All I could think of was "Wow! We're going to Florida!" I remember asking her, "What about Daddy?" And she just said, "Don't worry about it."

After we got there she put me in school, but since she didn't want to send for my school records, she started me in first grade instead of putting me in second grade, where I belonged. And I had to have all three of my shots over again, which I hated. The reason she couldn't write for my school records is because then my father might find out where I was and she didn't want that to happen.

School was really easy for me and I'd just sit there being bored. It seems like all we did was learn the alphabet, which I already knew, and play with blocks and do dumb things like that. I didn't have to stay for long, though, because one day my mother decided we were going to move without paying our next rent. We packed up all our belongings, climbed out the window, got in the car, and drove off. We slept in the car that night, and the next day we found a nice apartment. I went to another school, which was better because at least I was in second grade, where I belonged, but I didn't stay there for very long, either. One morning the principal came into my classroom and told me to pick up my stuff—to take some crayons and paper—because some man had come to pick me up. The man told me he was a detective and showed me a picture of my father. He asked me, "Do you remember this man?" And I said, "Yeah, he's my Dad." Before I knew what was happening we were driving off in his car, and

the next thing I knew I was in a courtroom and my father and my stepmother were both there. The judge decided that I should stay with my Mom for the time being so I wouldn't have to change schools, but my Dad and Kate could have me for the weekend. They had rented a motel room, so I left the courtroom with them.

That night we went out to eat with the detective, and the next day my father said he had two surprises for me. The first surprise was that we were going bowling, and later on he said that the second surprise was that we were all going to go on a big airplane. That's how I got to take my first plane ride—which was a lot of fun! The three of us flew back to New York and then went to my Dad's house—my old home—and that night we had a big party with lots of balloons and cake. Everyone was there—all my father's relatives and friends came and everyone was hugging me. The next week, my father appealed to the court in Florida and he won custody again, and this time he actually got to keep me because my mother didn't even try to get me back. It's hard to believe, but I haven't seen her since then, which is about four years now. At first I was glad because I was so happy to settle down and be in a good school, but then I started feeling sad, too, because I missed my mother. I still miss her.

When I think back over the past eight years, it seems as if I was just in one court and out the other, and half the time I didn't know what was going on. I went to about four different psychiatrists, but they didn't help, and the kids at school teased me when they found out I was going. Also, the doctors would always promise not to tell my father and new mother what I said, but a couple of them did tell, and anyway, who wants to talk to a total stranger about his problems? I don't. I just want to get on with my life and *forget* about what happened. Divorce is a very sad thing, but you get used to it after a while and thinking about it only makes it worse. I'm glad I'm where I am, but I wish people wouldn't talk about my mother, making her sound worse than she is. And when I talk to her on the phone, my father and stepmother always want to know what we talked about, and that upsets me. I know I can't go flying off to Florida every week—it's too expensive—but I hope we can work something out so I can see her again.

I feel guilty that my father and stepmother have so little money now, because I think it's my fault. I keep thinking that when I was in Florida maybe I should have told my teacher to call my father—or maybe I should have run away—so my Dad wouldn't have had to spend all his savings to track me down. He had to pay thirty-four thousand dollars for all the detectives, lawyers, and phone bills. But I was so young that I didn't know what was going on at the time.

Sometimes my Mom phones me and sometimes she writes me letters, but what I'd really like is the opportunity to see her and meet my two new half sisters. Even though I've gotten used to living without her and I've mostly forgotten what she looks like, I do think about her all the time. For a while I had a fantasy of running away to Florida, but that's pretty much died. I used to say things like "Mommy would do my homework for me" or "Mommy would let me stay up as late as I want—I could watch *Saturday Night Live* if I was in Florida."

Still, it really hurts me that my own mother hasn't been able to see me. She's always writing that she'll come up, but she never

makes it. She tells me it would cost too much money and that she's too busy with her kids. My father says that our top priority is getting our lives in order, but I do wish he could afford to send me down to Florida before I forget my first Mom completely. We might be able to go this year for my birthday, and I'm keeping my fingers crossed that everything will work out.

# *Sara, age twelve*

Two years ago we had to write an essay for our English class about a memorable day in our lives. This is what I wrote.

### A Troubled Heart

Today was special for me. I just got a 95 on a math test. My parents will be really proud of me. I had other reasons to be happy. In one week it would be my ninth birthday. Also, I had just made a new friend in school. I didn't have that many, since I just started school this year. I rushed home to tell my father the news. He works at home.

As I walked into the building I got this very strange feeling that something was wrong. I figured it was just the excitement of telling my father the good news.

Instead of getting my keys out and opening the door myself, I rang the doorbell so that I could tell him the news right away. I was greeted by my father. Before I had a chance to tell him anything, he started shouting at me for ringing the doorbell when I knew he was working. I was so startled and frightened I ran to my room and cried my heart out. He didn't even give me a chance to explain myself. This just didn't seem like Dad. Something must be wrong.

I stayed in my room the rest of the evening until my mother called me for dinner. I didn't say a word and neither did my parents. This proved that something was wrong.

After dinner I went back to my room and did my homework. I was still upset.

That night at about midnight I woke up to use the john. As I was walking down the hall I heard my parents fighting. My mother was crying. I ran back to my room and listened to their fight. I couldn't make out what they were saying, but I stayed up anyhow.

The next morning I was exhausted. As I dressed I noticed that no one else was up. I went into my parents' dressing room, and my mother was staring up at the ceiling. Dad wasn't there altogether. After I had checked all other possible sleeping places in the house, I asked Mom where Dad was. She replied that he had slept at Jack's house. Jack is a good friend of my Dad's. This was very strange but I didn't ask questions. As the day proceeded in school, it got harder and harder for me to concentrate. I couldn't stop thinking about why my Dad didn't sleep at home. Were my parents separating? Did they have a big fight? Or was Dad just working on something with Jack?

My friends saw how far away I was but didn't take much notice. My teachers didn't exactly enjoy it, either. I got yelled at twice for not paying attention.

Finally, when school ended, I was happy that the day was over but scared of what I might find at home. I tried to think of excuses for me to stay away from home for at least an hour or so. I decided to have a soda with a couple of friends. I called home and told my Dad, and before he could say anything, I hung up! When people decided to leave, I decided to face what might be waiting for me at home.

The bus ride home seemed really quick. As I entered the building, just as yesterday, I got this strange feeling. As I headed toward my front door I made sure to get out my keys and open the door myself. As I turned the key my mother opened the door. This was a shock, since she was never home when I got home from school. The first thing she said was "Your father has something to tell you." I walked very slowly. When I reached my father's working area I looked at him. He seemed very sad and solemn.

I sat down. Neither of us talked. We just sat there in silence until my father started to say something, but then he dropped it. He started soon again with "As you might have noticed, the atmosphere around here has been slightly strained and very uncomfortable lately."

I agreed and then he went on, "Your mother and I have decided to separate!"

We were both silent. After a couple of minutes I burst out in tears. I just cried, nothing else—didn't talk, didn't scream at Dad or Mom, didn't run out of the room. I just cried.

After I could control myself, I noticed that Dad was crying, too! I went over and hugged him, not for much of a reason but just because I loved him.

THE END

That day was three years ago.

After my father packed his bags and moved out, I was really upset and my mother was all depressed. It had a big effect on my life and for about two months I was fighting all the time with my Mom—about anything. About taking vitamins in the morning, eating breakfast, making my bed, keeping my room clean, doing my homework—dumb stuff like that. I used to scream at her, which was something I'd never done before. And I'd never heard her yell at me, either. It was because she was miserable and I was, too, but I didn't realize it at the time. It's only when I look back at it that I can see what was happening. Fortunately my parents knew what was going on, and they got me doing other things—like swimming at the Y after school—and soon we weren't fighting anymore.

It would probably help all kids going through a divorce to get involved in some after-school activity because it takes your mind off your school work and especially off your parents. The other advantage for me was that when we had swimming meets *both* my parents would come and it was nice for me to be able to see them together once in a while.

Another big problem, besides the constant fighting between my mother and me, was the money. It wasn't a critical situation, but it was annoying and it made me angry at Daddy. I'm sure he did his best, but my mother was paying for a lot of stuff which I felt was his responsibility. Fortunately, that's all been worked out now. Now that I'm older I can understand why they were having such money problems.

I guess the main reason I was mad at Daddy was because it all made my mother so unhappy, and I ended up feeling sorry for

both of them—my mother because she was struggling to make ends meet, and my Dad because he couldn't really do much about it.

Even though my parents separated more than three years ago, it's still very vivid in my mind and I doubt if I'll ever forget the way I felt at the time. Yet, as awful as it was, I never hoped they'd get back together. And now I think I'd die if they did, because it would be so awkward for me. I think they're both much happier now, and it's obvious to me that they both lead totally different lives. Since the breakup I've been able to see my parents' true colors, especially my mother's. I've seen a side of her that I never saw before. When she was married, she and Daddy were the perfect couple, always quiet, talking about dignified things, and they would never laugh or anything. Nowadays my mother is always happy and gay. Another way she's changed is that she always used to hide her problems from me but now she's more apt to discuss things. I think she's more relaxed—and so's my Dad.

Both of my parents started dating other people right away, and I think they'll both get remarried eventually, which is fine with me. They don't discuss their love lives with me all that much, but of course I'm not blind. For example, one night I had a sleep-over at a friend's house and the next morning I came home earlier than I'd planned to. Well, I just stormed into my mother's bedroom, and there was this guy in her bed—she was somewhere else, in another room. I started crying and everything, and my mother tried to convince me she had slept on the couch. Now that I look back, it was pretty hilarious, and of course I don't care—I mean, I understand about those kind of arrangements. In the beginning, when my father had a girlfriend sleep over, he didn't know how to tell me—he just sort of said, "Oh, you're sleeping on the couch tonight," because at that point I didn't have my own room at his house and shared the bedroom. It's still hard for my Dad to level with me about this part of his life, but he's getting better. Anyhow, neither of them should worry about my getting upset, because I'm old enough to understand that grown-ups are allowed to have private lives, which includes other people. But if someone's going to spend the night, I think it's better and less awkward if I know about it beforehand, so I'm not taken by surprise.

I still want to get married and have kids, but I have a lot of friends who don't want to. I was discussing marriage with one boy I know, and he said, "I'm never ever getting married." He took his parents' divorce really badly because his mother and father weren't friends afterwards—they were enemies, screaming on the phone to each other. I'm glad my parents are good friends, having lunch together and stuff. I think it's so much easier for the child if the parents are friendly. If they aren't, it's really difficult because there's always a right side and a wrong side and the kids are just caught in the middle.

I think I've grown up a little faster because of my parents' divorce. It's made me realize more about the problems of life and helped me to understand my parents—and appreciate them as individuals. It's just too bad they couldn't have been as happy and productive as a couple as they've been since they've been on their own. And I also wish that the next time my mother has tickets for a Rolling Stones concert, she takes me instead of her boyfriend, which is what she did the last time!

# *Kenny, age twelve*

I guess the main reason my parents got divorced is because they didn't fit together like they should. It wasn't that they hated each other. They simply grew too far apart and couldn't work it out anymore. I don't have any memories of their being together, because when they separated I was only two. I lived with my Mom and my two older sisters for the next seven years, and I'd see my father every other weekend—he'd come and pick us up on Friday night or Saturday morning and bring us back on Sunday night. I'm glad he spent a lot of time with us, because I can't imagine not having my father be part of my life. Another reason is, I'm very athletic and I enjoy doing sports with him. He'd practice with me and come to see all my football and soccer games at school.

When I was eight my mother remarried, and soon after that, my father also remarried. Up until then, Daddy had been renting a loft in Manhattan about an hour away from where the rest of us were living in Long Island. He and my stepmother, Nicky, bought a new house which was quite a bit further away, and it

was at this time that I decided I would like to live with him on a permanent basis. One weekend I asked him if it would be okay. I was a little worried that my mother's feelings would be hurt, and my Dad was, too, but I guess she figured that I should live where I'd be the happiest so she agreed. She knew my Dad loved us kids, and I think it made her happy that he had really participated in our lives and our upbringing and had always been there when we needed him. Since she knew I was doing what I wanted to do, I guess it was easier for her to accept my choice. What she didn't expect was that about a month later one of my sisters, Ronnie, also asked if she could move in with Daddy. Even my Dad was shocked, but that's what we did. Mom was probably scared that she was going to lose all three of us, but that didn't happen, because Lisa stayed with her. And actually she hasn't lost me or Ronnie—we're just not there as much as we used to be. My guess is that I'll stay where I am because I've made so many new friends here and because my Dad and Nicky and I really get along.

It's especially wonderful now because I have a brand-new baby sister, who's only two weeks old. Her name's Constance and I love taking care of her. Of course I can't help thinking how lucky she is that she's got these two parents who are staying together—parents who hold hands and who'll go to her class plays and go shopping together for her first bike. I'd say she's a little bit luckier than I am, with my parents divorced. I definitely think of Constance as my little sister—I wouldn't ever refer to her as my half sister. Same goes with Richie, my stepfather's son. We're only six months apart in age and we're like glue. On weekends when I visit my Mom, he's there visiting his Dad and we're never apart. He has an older brother and sister, and I do think of them as my stepbrother and stepsister because I don't know them as well.

All in all, I'd say my life hasn't been hurt too much by the divorce, and both my parents seem very happy and settled. If

anything's bothered me, it's been my religion's attitude toward divorce. I'm Roman Catholic, and besides being very active in my church—I'm an altar boy—I go to a parochial school, where most of my teachers are nuns. When my Mom and Dad got re-married, their marriages had to be performed by a judge instead of a priest, and that doesn't seem right to me. After all, the Catholic Church has been able to make some changes in recent years—like allowing girls to be altar boys—so I can't see why they can't be a little more broad-minded in their attitude toward divorce. People are going to keep on getting divorced no matter what. Just because their church says no, it doesn't mean they have to listen, and I think kids of divorced parents—Catholic kids, that is—would feel a lot happier if their church could rec-ognize not only divorce but remarriage as well. Being divorced is bad enough, but feeling God is mad too only adds to the feeling of guilt and makes the situation worse. For kids to go to school and be taught that divorce is a terrible thing—it's like being told that your parents are bad people and that they've offended God's feelings. Teachers are adding to the difficulty of being a single parent or a divorced parent. Nuns and priests in general should try to make it easier for kids of divorced families instead of making it worse—and if they make kids feel that their par-ents have done something wrong in God's eyes, that doesn't ex-actly help. It makes me very sad to think that when I get older I might have to drop out of the Catholic faith because it's not a comfort to me anymore.

# *Roberta, age fourteen*

I don't actually remember my parents' separating. I think I was six, but maybe I was only five. What I do remember is one particular fight they had around that time. It happened during the summer, when we were all on Fire Island, and my mother was so upset that she kept trying to call the police, but I kept pushing down the receiver so she'd have to redial. It's the only bad memory that I have, and even though it's still very painful to recall, now that I'm older I find it sort of silly because my father didn't seem to mind Mommy's making the call half as much as I did.

The main reason my parents got divorced is because they differed a lot in their opinions and there was a lot of conflict in what they thought about basic things. They're both architects and they used to work together, which caused additional stress, but they always seemed to get along, and except for that one fight I don't have any memories of them being mad at each other. Even now they get along really well—you know, sometimes I hear my parents on the phone and like my father will be laughing and I won't realize it's my mother he's talking to. I mean, from time to time it does strike me as strange that they get along so well for two people who couldn't live together. But I'm not old enough to realize that it *is* different when you do live together and operate as one unit. Now that they're apart and living separate lives, emotionally and professionally, they don't have anything to fight about.

Even though my parents are friendly and polite to each other, it never occurs to me that they might get back together. In fact, I wouldn't like it at all if they did. First of all, I wouldn't believe it. But mainly I've gotten used to things the way they are and now I'd have a hard time getting used to living with two parents at the same time. I can do things with my mother that I can't do with my father, and vice versa. For example, Daddy and I do a lot of sports together—like soccer and skiing. I tend to think of my father as a person to do things with and my mother more as someone to just *be* with—someone who takes a real interest in things I do on my own and who is real supportive of me. Another difference is that my father tends to like having lots of people around, whereas my Mom and I just go off by ourselves. My Mom's much more lenient about things like letting me watch TV, and when I got my ears pierced she didn't care but my father did. Actually, I'd like to get a third pierce but I know it would upset Daddy, so I'm going to wait until I'm older. Another difference is that my father has had a "constant companion" for the past seven years. Her name's Marian and she has two children from a previous marriage—a daughter, Emily, who's my age, and a son, Michael, who's twelve. Since Daddy and Marian aren't actually married and only live together dur-

ing the summer, Emily and I call each other "quarter sisters."
Mommy still lives alone and doesn't have a steady boyfriend.

The time I spend with each of my parents is very different, and
I really can't say I prefer one way of life to the other. All I know
for sure is that I like the change of pace. The way we've worked
things out is that my older brother, Alex, and I will both spend
a week with my mother at her home, and then the next week we
go to my Dad's. They live within a few blocks of each other, so
the switching back and forth hasn't presented any real problems.
Of course, there are times when I forget things, and it does mean
I have to carry a lot of stuff around, like my retainer and my
medicine for my allergies and extra clothes, but that doesn't
bother me, even if I do look like a shopping-bag lady whenever

I move from one house to the other. During the summer we alternate every six weeks, and we always spend Christmas with my father and Easter with my mother. On our birthdays it's whoever we're with and then the other parent calls. Alex and I stick together, and even though we don't always get along, he's made everything easier for me. He's older than me, so I've always felt I had somebody to fall back on if I needed anything. If he were younger, I don't know if I'd feel the same, but having an older brother to depend on has definitely been a big plus.

When my parents first got divorced, they had a different arrangement because Alex and I were so young and because they wanted to complicate our lives as little as possible. Instead of our moving back and forth, *they* did all the moving. It was really wonderful for my brother and me because we didn't have to do anything. My mother would come one week, and then she'd go stay at her office, where she had a bed and everything she needed, and my father would move in with us. We lived like this for a year or two, and, looking back, I think it made my brother and me feel very secure. I mean, they made it as easy as possible for us kids and I'm grateful to them for doing that. Maybe the fact that they'd been married for eighteen years and were both older—in their forties—made it possible for them to handle the divorce in a way that would disturb us as little as possible. Maybe if they had both been younger they wouldn't have known how to act as sensible as they did.

I do think that it would have been a harder adjustment if my parents had gotten divorced when I was in my teens, because I would have been used to them being together for longer. As it is, I can't imagine that I've missed anything by not having two parents at the same time, and it's probably made me a stronger person. I know it's changed my parents. My father has definitely grown a lot, because he's learned to cook, and my mother has expanded in other areas—she's more patient than she used to be. But the most important aspect of the divorce by far, and the reason my brother and I have been so lucky, is because each of our parents has been willing to take the responsibility of being two people—a mother and a father—when they're with us. I think if each parent can do that, then joint custody is a really good idea. The other thing that's made it easy for us is that they've never made us deliver messages back and forth. Neither of them has ever asked us to tell anything to the other parent unless it had to do with an appointment or something like that. It's possible I love them even more because of the divorce and the way they've worked things out without hurting Alex and me.

# *Tito, age eleven*

It seems like my parents were always fighting. The biggest fight happened one night when we were at a friend's house. Mommy was inside the house crying, and Daddy was out on the sidewalk yelling and telling my mother to come down, and my little sister, Melinda, and I were outside with a friend of my father's. We were both crying because we were so frightened. Then Daddy tried to break the door down, so Mommy came downstairs. And then the police cars came and Daddy begged Mommy to stay quiet and not say anything and to give him another chance, but she was so unhappy that she got into one of the cars. But just before she got into the car she came over to where we were standing, Melinda and I, and took us. That's when my father grabbed my arm and tried to take me back. He didn't want Mommy to leave and figured that if he could keep me, she'd have to stay, too. But the policeman took me and put me into the car on Mommy's lap. After Daddy realized that we weren't going to get out of the car, he went away, and after a little while Mommy and Melinda and I got out of the police car and went to a cousin's house. I was only four but I remember everything.

We stayed with our cousin for about two months, and during this time I saw my father whenever he visited us at my grandmother's house. Mommy didn't want to cut us off entirely from him because she worried that we might resent her if she did that. I was always happy to see him, but sometimes it made me feel sad, too, because I would look forward to our visits so much and then when we were together it could never be as perfect as I was hoping it would be. He was still so angry at Mommy's leaving him that it was hard for him to feel anything else for anybody.

He kept trying to talk her into coming back, and I really wanted them to get back together—I would beg her to try again because Daddy kept promising that he would change. But she didn't believe him, and this got me angry at her and made *her* look bad in my eyes. It's so weird because I realize now that it was my father who was causing most of the problems, but back then, as soon as he was away from us and there wasn't any fighting, I would get mad at my Mom for not letting him back. Now that I'm older I know that if she had let him come home we would have been right back where we were before, with all the fighting and violence. I guess I just missed him so much that I wanted him home. I kept begging Mommy, "Give him one more chance, and if he doesn't change, you can divorce him." But Mommy wouldn't change her mind and after a while we moved in with her mother. When I was six my parents finally got a divorce, and right after it was final my Dad moved to Puerto Rico. Since then I've hardly seen him at all. He's remarried now and has two children.

About the time of the divorce I started to get into fights with other kids, and my mother got worried. She thought I must be

feeling very angry and having a hard time expressing my feelings, so she took me to a therapist. His name was Dr. Gray and I saw him once a week after school. We got really close and he'd talk to me about my problems with my Dad. This went on for about two years, and during that time he helped me realize that the divorce was better for me in the long run because our home was more relaxed and there wasn't so much tension in the air.

The other thing that happened around this time was that my mother found out about an organization called Big Brothers, where I could have another male figure in my life—someone besides Dr. Gray. The way it works is that you go there and talk to a social worker, who matches you up with someone they think you'll be able to talk to and get along with. They paired me off with a guy named Pat Kelly, and we've been getting together every weekend for a couple of years. It's been great for me because my Mom tends to be too overprotective of me—she feels she has to be two parents—and I need a chance to get out on my

own. Pat and I do a lot of things like play baseball or video games and eat hot dogs. But the best thing we do is talk—like when I do something good in school I can tell him, and if I feel sad I can talk about that, too. His parents got divorced when he was twelve, and so we have a lot of the same feelings. Mostly, we talk about things that guys like to talk about—things like sports and girlfriends and personal stuff that I need advice on.

It makes me feel that I don't have to depend upon my mother a hundred percent of the time, and, best of all, that I don't have to feel so lonesome for my Dad. I still miss him, but at least there's someone who's like a father in my life, someone I can see and be with on a regular basis. Once in a while I think I'd like to move to Puerto Rico and live with my Daddy, but I doubt that will happen.

Even though Mommy got remarried last year, which means I have a new stepfather, I still feel closer to Pat in a lot of ways because we've had more time together and because I've never had to share him with my Mom. This past year has been very complicated but mostly very good. I'm getting to know my stepfather better every day, and I have a new house, new friends, a new school, and, as of two months ago, a brand-new baby brother. In a way I wish there hadn't been so many changes in one year, but I do feel happier than I've ever felt before. One good thing about the new baby is that Mommy has someone else to worry about, so she doesn't have to spend all her time worrying about Melinda and me. On the other hand, I have to admit that there are times when I feel jealous about all the attention the baby's getting. So I feel especially lucky to have Pat in my life. He's like my best friend—someone who's always there for me—and I don't have to share him with anybody. Sometimes I look at my little brother and I think that one day he'll be my age and I can be a big brother to him, playing ball and taking him to video parlors, and I hope I can be as good an influence on his life as Pat's been on mine. But most of all I hope that he won't have to experience all the pain and loneliness I went through when my parents got a divorce.

# *Corinne, age sixteen*

People ask me, "How does it feel to be divorced?" and I always say that I don't really seem to be affected by it because I was so young when it happened. The situation I have seems normal. Of course I'd like to live in the perfect house, with two dogs, a father, a mother, and all that, but I don't dwell on the idea. I make the best of the situation I have.

I was only two and a half when my parents separated. They split shortly after my younger brother, Randy, was born, and I know now how painful it must have been for my mother, having a newborn baby without a husband around. I only first realized what she went through a few years ago, when my grandmother told me what had happened. I was shocked, but instead of hating my father, it made me admire my mother all the more. I give her a lot of credit for not telling me. I'm sure a lot of mothers would have manipulated their children against the father, saying, "Your father did such and such." She never did that. In fact, the subject never came up until I asked my grandmother something about the divorce.

After my parents separated, my brother and I lived with our mother, and I can't remember seeing my father on a regular basis. I'm sure I saw him from time to time because I have photographs of us together, but I don't have any memories. He's always been very busy flying all over the place, so if we did see each other, it was probably something like once every two months.

I've never asked my parents why they got divorced or what their problems were. Sometimes I wonder what it was like when they were married, but they seem so different that I have a harder time imagining them together than apart. I'm glad I was so little when it happened because a lot of my friends who were older when their parents divorced have horrible memories of fighting and custody battles, and that was never a problem for me. To be honest, I don't think I was even aware that I was growing up in a divorced family until I was in elementary school and we had parents' visiting days. My father wouldn't be there and people would say, "Where's your Dad?" but I didn't care very much. I was getting along great with my Mom —I had no problems with her at all—and I didn't seem to be missing anything. Sometimes when I went to a friend's house where there was a mother and a father, I'd say, "Oh, that would be nice—it would be fun to have a perfect family," but I don't remember being upset about it. It certainly wasn't something that bothered me continuously. My life seemed so great that I didn't spend much time imagining how much greater it would be if a guy was there, too.

Now that I'm older I do think it would be good for my mother to find someone—I mean, I feel sorry for her because I'm always

going out on weekends and she hardly ever goes out. She's always kept herself very busy taking care of us and doing all sorts of things—serving on boards and committees, involving herself in our schools, and running her own flower business—but I feel that to a certain extent she's killing time with all these activities so as not to think about what she's *really* missing. She seems split in a way. Sometimes she says, "Oh, you guys are finally grown up, and when you've gone I can go live my own life and do what I want to do—I can move to the city and get my business really going," and at other times it's as if she's spending all her time with us because she can't seem to break the emotional tie. It's as if we represent a kind of security to her—the only kind of security she has.

My father, on the other hand, has been married four times— once before my mother, and then, when I was ten, he got married for about a year, maybe less. Now he's married to my present stepmother, Vana, and they've been together for about three and a half years. She and I have a great relationship—I'd say we're like sisters or very good friends—and I really enjoy her company. I never feel jealous of her because she's done so much for my Dad and he's so happy now. They don't have any children, and the truth is, I hope they don't have any. I guess I'm spoiled, but I have to admit this is something I feel strongly about. I would never want my father to have another child because then he might not have enough time to spend with my brother and me. We don't see that much of him now, and if he were busy taking care of someone else, we would see him even less. Of course it's not my decision—it would be up to him and my stepmother—but I think he'd value my opinion. Come to think of it, I guess you could say that the second big reason the divorce hasn't bothered me all that much is the fact that my brother and I haven't had to compete against any other kids for our parents' love and attention.

Still, it's been much tougher on Randy, who's had to grow up without a male figure in the house, even though my mother did an excellent job of playing both parts. She was always out there playing ball with him and going to all his games, but I know he's always felt very envious of his classmates with full-time fathers. And when he was little, neighborhood kids would say things like "Your Dad never cared" or "Your father left you," and I know he was very hurt by that. I know my brother would like to spend more time with Dad, and he's occasionally asked if he could go live with him, but my mother's always said no. In some ways she's very overprotective toward him. Everybody says he's my mother's little baby boy, and they may be right because she's always helping him with his homework and making sure nothing happens to him—and if she goes out, there has to be a baby-sitter even though he's thirteen years old and five-nine. Sometimes it's hard on me seeing him getting so much extra attention and time. I mean, I can understand why he does, because aside from his being a boy and missing a father figure, he's the youngest and it's hard for my mother to let go of him. But I worry for him because he's getting away with everything— like he gets to watch television until midnight and doesn't have to do his homework right away.

In a lot of ways I think it might be better for him to move in with Dad, because then he wouldn't be getting away with murder the way he is now. But I doubt it'll happen. First of all,

my mother still has the idea that my father is irresponsible and will never settle down—that he's too busy with his business and flying around. But the main reason is because I don't think my brother *really* wants to move. He likes the "idea," but he really prefers living with Mom because she's much more flexible. And he's pretty set in his ways, too. He's always saying stuff like "Oh, I never want to live with my Dad because I've got the best room in the world and I can't take my room with me—or my computer, or the icebox!" He's a real homebody—the type who gets homesick at camp—and it would be very difficult and painful for him to make such a change.

As for me, there are times when I think it would be great to live with my father, but then I realize it's too late now because I've got my friends and my high school and I don't want to leave them. I imagine that when I go off to college I'll be able to spend more time with him, like when I come home for vacations, and I'm looking forward to that. I'm just grateful that my Mom has given me such a good foundation. It's funny, but I see a lot of kids whose parents aren't divorced and somehow they don't seem as independent and self-assured as I am and a lot of them don't have as good a relationship with their parents as I have, so, strange as it might sound, I can't say that I have serious regrets about my parents' divorce. As for getting married someday myself, yes, I'd like to get married, and sure, I'd like it to last and have a golden wedding anniversary after fifty years, but life isn't perfect, and at least if it doesn't work out I can always say, "Well, divorce isn't all that bad as long as you can handle it in a way that doesn't hurt the children!"

# Caleb, age seven

My parents aren't actually divorced yet. But they're getting one soon. They stopped living together when I was one and a half, and my Dad moved next door. Then, when I was five, he moved to Chicago, and that hurt my feelings because I realized he was really leaving and I wouldn't be able to see him every day. My father's an artist, and when he lived next door to us in New York, I used to go to his studio every day and watch him when he was welding. I had my own goggles and tools, and we would spend many an hour together. I remember when I first heard the bad news that he was moving away, because I almost flipped my lid. My father said he would be divorcing my Mom but that he wouldn't be divorcing me and we'd still see each other a lot—but not as often. I started crying then and there, and ever since then I've been hoping every single second that he'd move back to New York and we'd all live together again. I don't cry much anymore because I hold it back, but I feel sad all the same.

I get to visit my father quite often. And Shaun. He's my collie. My cat lives in New York with me and Mom. Whenever I talk with Daddy on the phone I can hear Shaun barking in the background. The hardest thing for me about visiting my father is when I have to leave, and that makes me feel bad—and mad—inside. I still wish I could see him every day like I did when I was little. It's hard to live with just one person, because you don't have enough company, though my Mom has lots of great baby-sitters and that helps a little. Patrick Kilpatrick is one of my sitters, and it's comforting for me to have another guy around to do stuff with—like he takes me for rides on his bike and we play baseball together. We can do a lot more daredevil activities than I could ever do with my Mom. Patrick has never met my father, but sometimes we talk about him. He encourages me to talk about anything that's troubling me and reminds me I have a lot to be grateful for—like how great Mommy is and how I can visit my father whenever it's possible.

I hope my Mom never gets remarried because I just wouldn't like anybody else to try and take the place of my Dad. But sometimes when she's dating one man a lot and he's nice to me, I can't help wishing he was my Daddy. I told her that if she did ever want a husband, I have a list of choices and it would be nice if she could pick someone who could help me play with my computer. I wouldn't mind if my Daddy got remarried because maybe they'd have another kid and to tell you the truth I would really like to have a younger brother. But I wouldn't want my Mom to have a baby because it would live with us and then I'd have to share all my toys. Still, what I really really really want, deep down, is that my Dad doesn't get remarried and my Mom doesn't, either. What I'm just hoping and hoping more than anything is that they'll get back together again.

# *Heather, age eleven*

It's funny, because even though my parents were together until I was nine, I can't remember very much about that time at all. That's because there was so much bickering and so much hate that it's made me forget all the care they once had for each other. I can remember vacations but nothing about everyday life and how it was.

The really bad fighting started three years ago, at Christmastime. We always go to Cleveland to visit my grandparents, and this time I could tell something was bugging my Dad because he was at tight ends. Everything made him jump. Then, when we got home, my parents were always screaming and yelling at each other and crying and everything. So Mommy took me and Matthew—he's my younger brother—back to Cleveland. I figured we'd stay there for a couple of weeks until they solved their problems, and I think that's what my Dad thought, too, but then we enrolled in a new school and I figured we were staying.

During the time we were in Cleveland, Daddy came to visit us whenever he could, but since he didn't have anywhere to stay he'd just fly up in the morning and then leave at night. He didn't do it very often because it cost so much, but we'd call him once a week or he'd call us. It was really hard to talk to him because Matthew and I were both afraid to do something that might hurt Mommy's feelings.

We stayed in Cleveland for about six months—until June—and when we came back home Daddy was so happy to see us that he had tears coming down his face. By then my parents had decided to divorce, but neither one of them wanted to give up the house, so they continued living together for a while, and I think that's the dumbest thing they both ever did in their lives. It didn't work at all. After that, they tried alternating—leaving us at home and taking turns living with us. That didn't work either because my father would have the house one way and my mother would want it another way, and he wouldn't do her laundry and they both got different food. So there were *more* fights. Now they live in separate places—Daddy got the house and Mommy had to move out—and Matthew and I have been going back and forth for over a year. I hate it. I really do.

The way it works now is we switch houses every seven days—on Friday night at five-thirty. At first we tried switching every three days and that was crazy, and then we tried five days and that was still too confusing—one week we'd be switching on a Monday and the next week it would be Tuesday. And switching on school nights was awful. Friday nights are perfect because we don't have to worry about homework, and if Matthew and I both have after-school activities it doesn't matter because my Dad can take me and Mom can drive Matt. Another reason it works out well is because each of our parents likes to help

us with our homework and when we stay with them for a week at a time it's easier for them to keep up with what we're doing. If we switched every month, the parent who didn't have us would have a hard time keeping up. I'm very happy that both my mother and my father are so involved with our schoolwork.

So, if we have to switch back and forth, doing it on a weekly basis seems to work the best. And as long as they're divorced I don't see any alternative because it wouldn't seem right to live with either parent a hundred percent of the time and only see the other one on weekends. But switching is definitely the biggest drag in my life—like it's just so hard having two of everything. My rooms are so ugly because I never take the time to decorate them—I can't afford enough posters and I don't bother to set up my hair stuff in a special way because I know that I'll have to take it right back down and bring it to the next house. Now I'm thinking that I'll try to make one room my real room and have the other one like camping out. I can't buy two of everything, so I might as well have one good room that's really mine.

Another aspect of joint custody that's difficult is that my parents have very different rules and philosophies about life. For example, my Dad's attitude is that he lets us learn by our mistakes, and my mother does exactly the opposite—she tells us how to act before we make the mistake. And my Dad says we can watch TV for a while after school, and my Mom says we can't—that we have to select our programs very carefully. At my Dad's house Matthew has to do his homework right away, but he gets to stay up until nine and watch *The A Team* because that's his favorite show. Mom doesn't want him to when we're at her house but she feels she has to give in because Matthew says, "Well, Daddy lets me do that at his house." He's learning to play them against each other at a very early age. I don't do that, but I have to admit there are times when I secretly wish I was at whichever house I'm not at.

It would be nice if there could be a special house for divorced families. It would be like two houses, side by side, with a place in the middle where the kids could live. Then when parents had arguments they could each go to their own place and get away from each other and think things out by themselves. That way, they could realize how dumb they were behaving and get back together again. I know it's too late for that kind of arrangement with my parents—and as I look back I see that they're both happier being apart. My father's become a different person, you know, and it's unbelievable. I like the person he is now because he doesn't get angry as fast as he used to. And my mother's

much happier because she doesn't have to worry about getting Daddy mad. Another good thing that's happened is that my father's turned into a terrific cook, and it makes me feel proud to be one of the only people in my class whose father cooks and does things like taking me to hockey practice and to sewing. And it's great to see how my Mom doesn't have to rely on Daddy to pay the bills and throw out the garbage. She's working now and that's helped her feel important. Neither of them has to rely on the other one in dumb ways, the way they used to, and I think they're both much better off as a result. I know that neither of them will ever be able to forget all the anger, but I think that as time goes on they'll sort of come to their senses and be pretty good friends. That's what I hope for more than anything in the world!

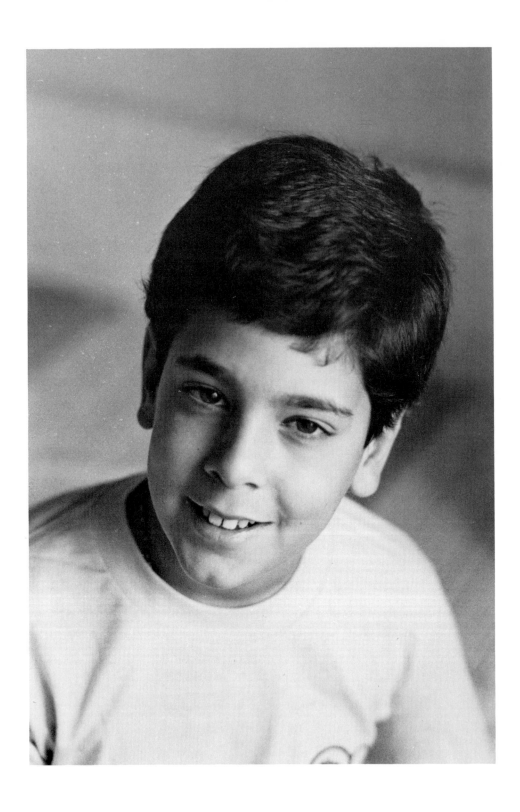

# *Daryl, age ten*

My parents were so young when they got married that they had trouble handling their problems. It was after I was born, when they started having a lot of arguments, that they realized they needed help, especially with me, and they turned to my Mom's parents for assistance. What happened is that I moved in with my grandparents when I was six months old, and I've been living with them ever since. It's been a perfect arrangement because Nana and Pop—that's what I call them—have already raised three kids, so they know how to take care of me. And besides, I've always been able to see my parents on a regular basis.

At first my mother and father didn't spend too much time with me because they were both like little kids themselves after the divorce. My mother was going through a real hard time emotionally and needed to get some professional help herself before she could be of much help to me. And my Dad was too young and irresponsible then to be a good father. In fact, I hardly saw him at all except on my birthdays. I remember one time I was playing soccer and all of a sudden after the game was over this

guy with a mustache comes up and says something like "Well, how are you playing?" and I say, "Okay," and then he says, "Do you know who I am?" and I say, "No." "Well," he says, "I'm your father." I could hardly believe it! But I don't hold it against him at all, and now I see him quite often and it's great. I think that if I hadn't been getting the love and attention I needed from my grandparents it would be easy to be mad at him, but the way things are, I'm just glad that he had the time he needed to get his life together.

Now that I'm older and my parents are more grown up themselves, they're more involved with me. I realize how when I was born neither one of them was ready for marriage or for children and it was just very lucky for everyone that my grandparents wanted me. In many ways it's especially been lucky for them, too. My grandfather says I've kept him young and in good shape because we do a lot of sports together—he even got a baseball mitt so he could practice with me. As for Nana, she's always on her feet doing something—like baking up a storm for the bake sale at my school—and this year she's the head class mother. She's a real character in a lot of ways. She signs all my report cards: GRANDMOTHER AT LARGE . . . IN CHARGE. I'd definitely say that my grandparents do everything that other kids' parents do. It might have been difficult for them when I was little, but now that I'm older it's easier because I do a lot of jobs around the house and don't need help as much as I used to.

I have a hunch that in a year or so my Mom will move in with us and that she's going to take more charge of me, but Nana will still be in charge of the house. They get along well, so I imagine it'll all work out. I know that I wouldn't want to move, because I've grown used to things the way they are—I love my room, and my friends, and my school, and, most of all, I love my grandparents. I've had such a wonderful life with them that I've never wasted time worrying about what might have happened if my parents hadn't gotten divorced. And now that my mother's back on her feet I'm not going to worry about what's going to happen if she wants me back. It seems she's always done what's best for me, and I'm sure she'll want me to continue my life the way I like it—and that's the way it is now!

# Nancy, age fifteen

It happened very gradually. Five years ago my parents separated, but it was only a separation within the house—my Dad just moved into another bedroom—and they tried to keep it from my sister, brother, and me for about a year. I don't think my younger brother and sister caught on, but I knew my Dad was sleeping in the other room and I knew they were having problems. Still, I wasn't really affected because it wasn't hurting me in any way. They were arguing so much that I kind of *wanted* them to get it over with as long as we could all be happy, and I figured we'd all be happier if they were apart. In fact, everything was fine for a while—until they started involving me, and then it was terrible. My mother would say, "Go tell your father this or that," and then he'd give me some message to give to her, and it seemed like they were putting all their problems—anything that was on their minds—on me. Even when I complained, it didn't help, because they still had a way of keeping me in the middle. I'd say, "I'm not going to deal with this—it's *your* problem, it's *your* life," but then they'd only get annoyed at me. I always felt that I had to solve everything for them. Life got a lot better after they finally sold the house, but that was very painful for us kids, too, because that's where we grew up and now we don't feel that we have a real home anymore. But anything's better than having to hear my parents fighting.

I think that if parents are going to divorce and not scar their children for life, they should keep them out of what's going on as much as possible. I'm not saying parents should lie to kids or anything, but they shouldn't make them suffer for what they've done and they don't have to give them all the details of what went wrong. Or try to make them hate the other parent. One of the reasons I may have bad feelings now toward my mother is that I feel she tried to turn me against my father.

Being the oldest child, I tried to help in the beginning, but then I realized they were only using me. It got to the point where I was so unhappy I couldn't study. My grades were falling and I got so worn down that I'd fall asleep in classes. It was such a bad time for my mother that she starting holding on to me for her own security, and I felt as if she was pulling me down with her. My father was using me, too. It was as if I was the only one they depended on, when they should have been depending on their lawyers.

Finally I asked my Dad if I could go to a doctor—a child psychiatrist— to sort out my problems, and he said he thought it would be a good idea. Looking back, I think it was Dr. Schwartzberg who pulled me through. Without his help I would probably have turned to drugs or liquor because they would have been my only means to escape from all the problems I had. I needed to escape somehow, and it's not as though I was free to just walk

out of the house. I think that when parents are getting divorced it's smart for the kids to go see someone, and I think they should understand that this doesn't mean they're crazy. It's stupid for anyone to say "I don't need a psychiatrist—they're for crazy people," because that's not true. It just helps you to understand yourself and your problems.

My mother and I were having such terrible problems that I moved in with my father for a while. My doctor told me that my mother was probably feeling a little jealous of me because I still had my Dad and his love, and that because I was the oldest girl in the family she was probably taking it out on me. During this whole time my mother seemed almost reluctant to touch me and kind of cold, and it was impossible for us to talk comfortably. But when I wanted to leave the house she would cry and tell me how much she needed me. It was very painful for me because children need their mothers and my mother isn't a bad mother. When we were younger she used to be wonderful and she gave me a real good base and a good study atmosphere, but the divorce really messed things up and it got to be very hard for her to keep on being as good a mother because she was so unhappy.

Dr. Schwartzberg told me that I had to separate the past from what was happening now and that I had to realize what was best for *me*—that I shouldn't worry about hurting my parents' feelings. He thought that it might be a good idea for me to go away to boarding school so I could settle down and get back to concentrating on my schoolwork. And he thought it was important for me to stop worrying so much about my brother and sister. So that's what I did, and the last year has been much

easier. My grades are up again and I've been able to make a lot of new friends.

Recently my father remarried and we're all very happy about it. There are times when I get a little jealous of my Dad's new wife because she's getting a lot of the attention I used to get, but I'm happier when she's around than when she's not. I tried to explain to my Dad that I could love her and still feel jealous and that I wasn't going to try to compete with her, but of course he wants everything to be too perfect. At least he's learning to listen to me and value my opinions. As for my mother, we're getting along a lot better now. She's got a boyfriend and a new job and she's feeling happy again. She was such a good mother when we were little, and it's wonderful to see her getting to the point where she can be a really good mother once again.

# *Malik, age fourteen*

I've lived with my mother all my life. My parents got divorced when I was one year old, and I guess I was about eight when I started seeing my father on weekends. I'd go visit my grandmother and he would come over, but I didn't see him unless I was at her house. Now that I'm older I see him on a fairly regular basis. He's happily remarried now—to his third wife—and he and my stepmother have a nine-year-old daughter named Laurie. Even though I like Laurie and we have plenty of fun together, there are times when I feel jealous of her because she does seem to get the lion's share of everything—for example, she gets more new clothes and presents than I do. She's treated as though she's queen of the ball. It's hard for me not to feel that my father loves my little sister more than me, and that makes me feel both sad and mad. Sometimes I try to talk to him about it, but he just tells me that my stepmother buys all those things for her and that it's not his fault.

I'd say that one of the most difficult aspects of divorce for me is that my mother's so busy working at her job and running the house that by the end of the day she's too tired to do things with me. There are times when I can't go to a party or a friend's house because she doesn't want to stay up until ten or eleven in order to pick me up. On top of that, she worries about my being out after dark because, as she says, I'm all she's got. It would be much easier if I could call on my Dad from time to time, but he works pretty hard, too, and now that he has his own family responsibilities I can't rely on him. I wish I could because I do think it's up to him to help my Mom when it involves doing things that I still can't do for myself.

Some of the advantages of my parents having gotten their divorce when I was so little are that I didn't have to go through hearing them argue and I never got very attached to my Dad, so when he left I didn't miss him all that much. Sometimes we go on trips together—like to the Poconos—but most of the time he's like any "weekend father" in that I don't think about him too much during the week. I'm too busy thinking about what's going on at home, and home to me is where Mom and I live. But the really wonderful thing that's happened to me is that since I've never had much of a family life, so to speak, I spend a good deal of time by myself, and have gotten very involved in art. I spend hours and hours drawing and I can get totally lost in it.

Sometimes I feel that I'm a little bogged down with all the extra responsibilities that have come my way, since I'm the only male around. You know, I vacuum, clean the bathroom, take out the garbage—whatever my mother tells me to do. But since I can't tell *her* what to do, I never really feel like the man of the house. I feel like the son.

Sometimes I think it would be good if my mother got remarried. It's hard to go to your mother for advice about things, and sometimes my father isn't available, although he tries hard when he's around. Also, to tell the truth, it's hard living with just one person. There's no appeal system—your mother says no, and there's no father to go to, hoping he'll say yes!

# *Tracy, age sixteen*

I'm the youngest of six, so my parents' divorce really took me by surprise. Since I was the baby of the family, everyone tried to protect me from what was really going on, but after a while even I realized that they weren't getting along, and after that I wanted them to separate. I actually hoped they would get a divorce. One time the fighting got so bad that my sister had to call the police.

The last couple of years have been really painful for me because I've tried so hard to have a good relationship with my father and it hasn't worked out very well. He only visits us about once a year, and because I hardly ever see him I always feel that I have to be on my best behavior and it's hard to be natural. Sometimes he tries to manipulate me by making me feel guilty about always siding with my Mom. Trouble is, I do end up feeling guilty, when *he's* the one who's acting badly. The other thing he'll do that will hurt feelings is he'll say something like "You're just like your mother" when he's being negative. That hurts a lot.

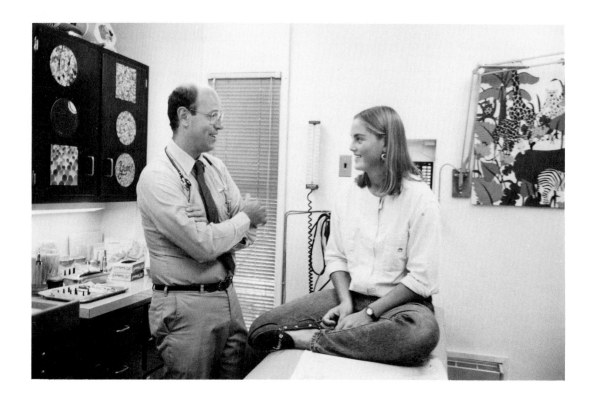

Even though I thought the divorce was a good idea, it still made me feel sick inside for the first few years. I cried a lot—like whenever I would see my Dad I would come home afterwards and cry hysterically. I was so sick that I'd throw up, and it got to the point where I had to stay out of school for two months. They did all these tests on me to see if I had something wrong with my stomach, but the doctor said it was just the pressure and tension I was under. During this time my pediatrician was extremely helpful and was the person I ended up talking to about my problems. And then this past year I went to a psychotherapist once a week, and she was very helpful, too, especially with regard to all my guilty feeling about not being able to get things going with my Dad. She showed me that I don't have to love someone just because he's my parent—that he has to *earn* my respect and be nice and show me he wants to have a *real* relationship, not just suddenly become my best pal whenever we happen to get together. This past year I think I've really been able to go inside myself, and it has made me toughen out a lot. It's also made me more understanding. I suggested to my Dad that we try to make something consistent—like writing to each other once a month—but he just said, "Sure," and then he never did it. Now I finally realize that I'm probably better off settling for a limited relationship.

Both my parents have remarried, but I'm not too close to either of my step-parents. I've only met my father's wife twice, so I hardly know her. But I'm not all that close to my mother's husband either, even though I live with both of them. I like him but I don't go out of my way to be friendly. I respect my Mom's right to remarry—I have to. But I was still upset because I worried that I would be losing her. I felt that I had supported her through the whole divorce and that after our spending so much time together I'd be losing time with her and she would love someone else besides me.

But the worst thing by far about my parents' divorce is that it's still going on. I mean, my parents don't talk. If they have to talk, it's like screaming. I thought that once the divorce was over, my Mom and Dad could just get on with their lives, but it hasn't worked out that way. I think that the fighting will never stop.

# Nelson, age sixteen

I can barely remember when my parents were together. I only have dim memories because I was three or four when they got divorced. My little sister had just been born, so their divorce seems especially weird. I mean, God, it's so hard for me to imagine how people who've just had a baby can turn around and split up.

When my parents were first getting divorced they used to have the most terrible fights on the phone which I can still remember vividly—they would have these violent conversations which were mostly about money. So, one thing you can be sure of is that I was never one of those "divorced kids" who kept hoping their parents would get back together, because when I saw the way they fought, I was just glad there was a phone line separating them. I didn't even want them in the same house. Sometimes I look at pictures of them together, back in the 1960s, and I cannot imagine why they ever got married in the first place. It's one of the mysteries of my life.

I don't recall being all that upset about the divorce, but around the time I was five, I was going to school and my teacher thought

I was acting a little strange. What happened is that one day all the kids in my class were dancing around, pretending they were seagulls, and I just said to myself, "Oh God, I'm not going to do that," so I just sort of sat down and read a book. When my parents heard about this incident they were convinced that I was upset about my family life, and they sent me to a child psychiatrist. So I'd go and see this guy and we'd talk and play checkers, but I never did feel that I was as upset by the divorce as I was about having to pretend that I was a seagull.

What actually helped me more than the psychiatrist was the fact that I had a sister, because that meant there was always someone there, someone for me to be with when my parents were fighting. My sister was probably affected a lot less than I was because she was too young to really understand what was going on, but I did know what was happening and I was very relieved that I never had to be alone while they were battling it out. Fortunately, the fighting stopped around four or five years ago. I don't know why, but I guess they finally settled their differences—or got sick of fighting. Or maybe they just mellowed out a bit.

We have a joint-custody arrangement and divide our time fairly equally with each parent. They live close enough to one another that my sister and I can switch back and forth without too much trouble. Since I always see my parents separately, I probably perceive them more as individuals and less as "parents" and I can understand their problems. For example, even though my mother works, and always has, she's often too wrapped up in her problems to, shall we say, efficiently discipline me. It's not that she's all that unhappy, but sometimes she feels frustrated she has to take a teaching job in addition to her free-lance writing, and then there's the fact that she can't seem to find anybody. You know, at times it's as though life becomes almost too much for her, and this can make her a much less effective parent. My father, on the other hand, is more strong-willed, but he also has his weaknesses, which are that he's way too overbearing, too bossy—like if I want to do something and he wants me to do something else, he may say, "Why don't you do this?" but then there's this undercurrent of "You do it or else!" That's one thing I don't like. Nevertheless, I really love each of my parents and I get along with them wonderfully. And even though they got divorced, my childhood memories are happy ones. What I mostly remember are the summers I had with each of them and how fantastic everything was. It seemed that when I was young, there was nothing evil in the world and that everything was bright and sunny.

I do think that when parents divorce they should make it very clear to their kids what they're doing, but somehow they should keep their kids away from all their emotional fighting with each other. If they knew how their fighting affected their children, I think parents would make a bigger effort to do this. And they shouldn't make their kids message-carriers either. The best advice I could give other "divorced" kids is to stay out of it when your parents fight. Don't sit there and listen. Leave! Go to a different room or leave the house altogether. Go anywhere. It doesn't matter where, as long as you get the hell out of there. And if they try to use you as a messenger, tell them that if they want to speak to each other, to do it directly and leave you alone.

The most profound effect my parents' divorce has had on me is that I'm really going to think twice before I ever get married.

Breaking up is a much bigger deal if you're married than if you're only living together. My father's remarried now, but before he met his present wife he lived for a while with another woman, and in some ways I think their breaking up probably affected me more than it did them—it was actually almost a bigger shock to me than when my parents got divorced. However, when they both decided it wouldn't work, she was gone in a week—no fights, no alimony, no child support, no great emotional hazards.

I don't mean to say that I'm sorry my parents got married, because I'm not. As divorces go, theirs hasn't been all that bad. I've been able to have a good continuing relationship with both my mother and my father, and I've also been able to keep on living in the same place where I grew up. One of my greatest childhood fears was that my mother would have to move and I wouldn't have my same room anymore. I loved my room and I was really paranoid that my mother would move, either because she was unsatisfied with the apartment or because she would get married again. But I guess the main reason I'm glad they got married is because they had me and my sister, and I'm very glad that we were both born!

# Gillian, age thirteen

I was about four when my parents got divorced, and I don't remember anything that happened that year. It's like a total blank. I remember things that happened to me before then and afterwards, but it's like I have amnesia around the time they split up. No one believes me, but I do remember lots of things that happened to me *before* the divorce—from when I was really little. I can remember living in Holland when I was one, and I vividly remember parts of our house—like my brother's room and our stairway. We moved to Germany when I was two, and I remember even more about the year we spent there—things like going through my sister's toy chest and riding around the living room on my tricycle while my family clapped. The memories of those first three years are so important and precious to me that I guess I've always wanted to hold on to them. I hope I'll never forget them. Those are the years that Mommy and Daddy were still married.

From the time my parents got divorced until I was eleven, which is when my father got remarried, I always had the same wish whenever I blew out the candles on my birthday cake. I always wished that my parents would get back together again. For a long time I worried that I had actually caused the breakup, because whenever I did anything my older sister didn't like, she'd tell me that *I* was the reason my parents got divorced, that it was all my fault and if I hadn't been born they'd still be together. I'd cry and cry, but I'd never ask Mom or Dad if it was true—not because I subconsciously might have thought my sister was right, but mainly because I never really faced their divorce head-on. I just hung on to the notion that they'd get back together again.

One of the most painful consequences of the divorce for me has been that it's been hard to have an easygoing relationship with my mother. After Daddy moved out, I think she expected more of me—you know, being a perfect daughter and getting good report cards all the time. And it made her worry about money all the time, too. I always felt as though I was caught in the middle, and I resented that. Mommy would say things like "If you want to go to gymnastics class, you'll have to ask your father to pay for it," and Daddy would say, "You shouldn't be in the middle of this. If your mother wants me to pay for something, then she should call me." But of course he was making me the middleman, too, because I'd have to relay his message to her. Whenever I talked to either parent, it was like being on the telephone with someone who really wants to be speaking to someone else. If parents are going to get divorced in the first place, they should expect to pay the consequences, which include talking directly to each other—even if they hate each other. The kids shouldn't be dragged into their problems.

And I had enough problems just shuttling back and forth between two very different households. I hated going back and forth between my father's house and my mother's house, and I often asked myself—and them—why they couldn't live together again. It wasn't until after Dad married Meg that it dawned on me that if my parents had gotten remarried to each other they would have been miserable, which wouldn't have made my life very happy either!

Dad and Meg have a new baby, Jocelyn, whom I love very much. But I have to admit I'm envious of her—not jealous, but envious that she gets to have a full-time Daddy. She's really lucky that every year of her life, until she goes away to college, her Daddy will be there—you know, when she learns to throw a ball or write her name. Whenever she does something for the first time, he'll be there. It makes me sad that Daddy hasn't been there for me full-time for the past ten years of my life.

A year ago my mother got remarried—to Bert—and it's been hard for me to adjust because we had to move into his apartment. I felt as if Mother had taken me out of my own home and put me into another place which she wanted me to think of as my home but which I really thought of as Bert's house. I only stayed there for a year, though, because I really wanted to live with Daddy and Meg, and so that's where I've been staying for this past year. It's much better for everybody, and I'm a lot happier. It's especially improved my relationship with Mommy—I spend every weekend with her—because now she's much more relaxed. Maybe it's because she doesn't feel so responsible for my actions—like if I don't do well on a test, she doesn't feel that it's *her* fault. We're much closer than we've ever been because we don't fight anymore.

My Bat Mitzvah was nice because it gave me a chance to have some memories of an occasion with both my mother and father there. We even have a picture of all five of us, with me standing between Mommy and Daddy. The last time I remember them together is when I was three.

When parents divorce, I think everybody underestimates the child's mentality. Parents say things like "Oh, I know what's best for her—she doesn't really know," but it's not true. If a child wants to stay with his father or mother, there's a reason for it and parents should *listen* instead of doing all the talking.

I don't want to get married when I grow up because I don't want to get divorced. Not ever. You see, if I did marry I'd probably have a kid, and I wouldn't want to put somebody I loved in the position I'm in now. If you ask me, the real problem for

anyone getting married these days is that divorce is such an easy out. I don't really know if I want to get married under conditions where if we have a fight or if my husband doesn't like the way I act around other people, all he has to do is ask me for a divorce. It's so stupid. I truly believe that most situations can be worked out—and ought to be. Divorce is like suicide. Instead of trying to solve their problems, people just kill their marriage because it's the easy way out.

It's still hard for me to say anything to my parents if something upsets me. Writing poetry has always been the best way for me to get my feelings out. That way, no one can get mad at me and things don't stay all bottled up inside of me, either. I have a big box with a lock on it where I keep all my writing. I've probably written over a hundred poems so far. These are a few of my favorites:

*Why couldn't they stay together?*
*Like two dying stars—*
*Waiting till all was right to end it,*
*Waiting till I understood?*
*But no—*
*Like the sun and the moon*
*They split*
*Leaving me to be earth*
*Solid as they were not.*

*Like the Red Sea*
*Parted*
*Yet never joined again*
*Mommy's world*
*Daddy's world*
*So different*
*Sometimes I wonder*
*Which is better for me?*
*But I'll never really know.*

*I used to dream they'd marry again*
*They didn't*
*I used to dream everything was all right*
*It wasn't*
*I used to dream I was happy*
*I wasn't.*

# *Bartle, age twelve*

We were on vacation when my Dad told me that Mum would be moving out and getting her own apartment. I was only eight years old at the time, and even though no one used the word *divorce*, I knew what was happening—not that I'd had any suspicion that it was coming. I didn't. I had no idea because I never saw them acting in any way that would have indicated they weren't getting along. It's not as if they ever had any big fights or anything. After he had told me, I put my arms around him and said, "I feel sorry for you, Daddy." We both cried for about two hours.

I do think that divorce can be more difficult for an only child because it's easier if you have other people to talk to. But I'm luckier than most kids because I can really talk to my parents. They're good listeners, and no matter what's on my mind—even if it's dumb—they really pay attention and try to help me.

For a long time I hoped they'd get back together, but I know it's impossible. I still wish it wasn't but they're just so different it probably wouldn't be good for anyone. I was so young when they got divorced that I've never really known what my life would be like if they were together. It's like being a horse with blinders on—the horse only sees what's in his line of vision, and he doesn't see, or even imagine, anything else.

As things are now, we have a great arrangement. I stay six months of the year with my Mum, six months with my Dad, and I alternate weekends, so I'm never really away from either of them for very long. Of course, there are times when things get switched around, but that's the basic structure and I'm very happy with it. Lots of divorced kids at my school have come up to me and said, "What kind of deal do you have with your parents—I hear it's pretty good," and so I tell them. One of my friends even got his parents to try a similar arrangement. Unlike other divorced families, I don't feel I've lost one of my parents.

I like dividing my time equally between my parents, and I know they're happy about it, too. One advantage of this arrangement is that I'm really close to both of them and I've gotten to know them really well as friends. I'm probably much closer to my Dad than most kids are to their fathers. He makes me feel that he *really* enjoys being with me, that it's not just an obligation.

One of things I do a lot with both my parents is reading. There's no TV set at all in my Dad's apartment, and almost every night we read out loud together, usually Arthur Conan Doyle. And my Mum and I often read out loud in French.

Sometimes my dog can be a problem—his name is Ralph and he sticks with me—but that's the kind of problem we can work out. When I was younger, one good part about moving back and

forth was that it was a great excuse if I wasn't able to do my homework. You know, I'd say I left it at my Dad's, and instead of getting mad, the teacher would usually say something like "Oh, you're divorced," and instead of getting mad, he or she started feeling sorry for me.

But, to be serious, there are a few things that are still very difficult and painful for me—like having to act like a middleman, taking messages back and forth. On the other hand, that's better than hearing them argue over the phone. One time they were having an argument and my Mum accidentally left the answering machine on, and afterwards when she played it back and heard herself she said, "Oh, God, I'm so stupid!" She said she'd really been wrong, and I think it helped her a lot. It would probably be a good thing for all divorced parents to be able to play back their telephone conversations.

Another thing that's hard for me is seeing the difference in my Mum's life-style now that she's living on her own. She's got a great job, but since the divorce she's had to be much more careful about how she spends money. My Dad, on the other hand, hasn't had to make any real compromises.

But the most painful thing by far has been dealing with my parents' dating other people. They try to include me—like having me join them when they go out for dinner—but I have to admit that sometimes I sit there and feel that I'm not getting enough attention. I feel jealous, and then I end up feeling guilty because even though I know I'm entitled to my feelings, I also know I'm being unfair to everyone. I'm hoping it will get easier for me as I get older, because I don't like having these feelings at all.

All in all, I think that when your parents divorce, it gives you a broader view, a wider scope, because you do get to know each parent a lot better and you see two different views of life. On the other hand, sometimes I think that maybe the divorce is making me grow up too fast. I'm only twelve but sometimes I think I'm as grown up as either of them!

Special thanks to:

Betsey Jayne, Lois Cunniff, Rabbi Daniel S. Wolk, Carole Versace, Dr. George Reed, Mel Scott, Maily Smith, and Dianne Kane, Director of Social Work at Big Brothers Inc., who put me in touch with many of the young people in this book.

Dr. Peter F. Wohlauer, Dr. Arnold Cooper, and Linda Bird Francke for their insights and encouragement.

Carol Atkinson, who, as always, transcribed all the tapes from my interviews with speed and intelligence.

Eugene Merinov, who printed the photographs.

Bob Marceca, who rented me a quiet and wonderful office so I could finish this book.

Everyone at Knopf, especially my editor Bob Gottlieb, and John Woodside, Martha Kaplan, Mary Maguire, Tasha Hall, Andy Hughes, and Sara Eisenman.

J.K.

A NOTE ON THE TYPE

*This book was set on the Linotype in Granjon, a type named in compliment to Robert Granjon, typecutter and printer active in Antwerp, Lyons, Rome, and Paris from 1523 to 1590. Granjon was designed by George W. Jones, who based his drawings on a face used by Claude Garamond (1510–1561) in his beautiful French books. Granjon more closely resembles Garamond's own type than do any of the various modern faces that bear his name.*

*Composed by Maryland Linotype Co., Baltimore, Maryland. Printed and bound by Halliday Lithographers, Hanover, Massachusetts.*

*The design of this book is based on designs by Sara Reynolds and Dorothy Schmiderer.*